Easy Cookbooks for Kids

Easy Lunches From Around the World

Sheila Griffin Llanas

Enslow Elementary

Library of Congress Cataloging-in-Publication Data

Llanas, Sheila Griffin, 1958–
  Easy lunches from around the world / Sheila Griffin Llanas.
    p. cm. — (Easy cookbooks for kids)
  Includes index.
  Summary: "Make simple lunch items from different countries"
  —Provided by publisher.
  ISBN 978-0-7660-3708-3
  1. Luncheons—Juvenile literature. 2. International cooking—
Juvenile literature. 3. Quick and easy cooking—Juvenile literature.
4. Cookbooks. I. Title.
  TX735.L74 2011   2010037759
  641.5'55—dc22

Paperback ISBN 978-1-59845-272-3

Printed in China
052011 Leo Paper Group, Heshan City, Guangdong, China
10 9 8 7 6 5 4 3 2 1

To Our Readers: We have done our best to make sure all Internet addresses in this book were active and appropriate when we went to press. However, the author and the publisher have no control over and assume no liability for the material available on those Internet sites or on other Web sites they may link to. Any comments or suggestions can be sent by e-mail to comments@enslow.com or to the address on the back cover.

Every effort has been made to locate all copyright holders of material used in this book. If any errors or omissions have occurred, corrections will be made in future editions of this book.

Illustration Credits: All photos are from Shutterstock.com, except as noted.
© Bon Appetit / Alamy, p. 32 (pyttipanna); © Lenscap /Alamy, p. 46 (Vegemite); © Panacea Pictures /Alamy, p. 46 (Marmite); ©1999 Artville, LLC, (all maps) pp.14, 17, 20, 23, 26, 29, 32, 35, 38, 41, 44; ©2011 Photos.com, a division of Getty Images. All rights reserved., p. 11 (vegetable peeler); ©Aleaimage/iStockphoto.com, p. 41 (corn and shrimp soup); ©Clipart.com., pp. 8, 9; ©Nicole DiMella/Enslow Publishers, Inc., p. 35 (sauerkraut soup), p. 38 (arepas), p. 39 (flour), p. 44 (mousetraps); Courtesy of NomNom Truck.com, p. 26 (bánh mì sandwich); iStockphoto.com/© Fenykepez, p. 36 (paprika peppers); iStockphoto.com/© Jim Jurica, p. 18 (salsa in bowl); iStockphoto.com/©Don Nichols p. 10 (cookie sheet); United States Department of Agriculture (USDA), p. 12

Cover Illustration: iStockphoto.com/©AVAVA

<u>Warning:</u> The recipes in this book contain
ingredients to which people may be allergic
such as peanuts, dairy products, and shellfi

Contents

Introduction

In Belgium and Holland, people dip their French fries in mayonnaise. In Bulgaria, pizza is topped with a dab of mustard or ketchup. In Sweden, pickles go with eggs and potatoes. It is fun to learn what people eat in other countries. Some foods might sound strange until you taste them! You might find new flavors that you enjoy and new dishes you love to cook and eat.

As you use this cookbook, you will learn about countries around the world. Eleven recipes come from eleven different regions, one from each. When you follow a recipe, you can read about the country the dish comes from and the special ingredients that flavor it.

Each recipe in this book has specific directions on WHAT YOU NEED and WHAT TO DO. You will also find cooking tips. The tips help you to be safe and have fun in the kitchen. They will make you a more skillful chef.

Be Safe!

Whenever you are in the kitchen, there are important safety rules to follow:

1. Always **ask a responsible adult** for permission before starting to cook. Always have an adult by your side when you use the oven, the stove, knives, or any appliance.

2. If you long hair, tie it back. Remove dangling jewelry and tuck in any loose clothing.

3. Always use pot holders or oven mitts when handling anything on the stove or in the oven.

4. Never rush while cutting ingredients. you don't want the knife to slip.

5. If you are cooking something in the oven, stay in the house. Always use a timer—and stay where you can hear it.

6. If you are cooking something on the stove, stay in the kitchen.

7. ALLERGY ALERT! If you are cooking for someone else, let them know what ingredients you are using. Some people have life-threatening allergies to foods such as peanuts, dairy products, and shellfish.

Cooking Tips and Tricks

Keeping Clean:

- Wash your hands before you start. Make sure to also wash your hands after touching raw poultry, meat, or seafood and cracking eggs. These ingredients may have harmful germs that can make you very sick. Wash knives and cutting boards with soap and water after they've touched these ingredients.

- Use two cutting boards (one for meat and one for everything else) to avoid getting any germs from the meat on other food.

- Rinse all fruits and vegetables under cool water before you use them.

- Make sure your work space is clean before you start.

- Clean up as you cook.

Planning Ahead:

- Read the recipe from beginning to end before you start cooking. Make sure that you have all the ingredients and tools you will need before you start.

- If you don't understand something in a recipe, ask an adult for help.

Measuring:

- To measure dry ingredients, such as flour and sugar, dip the correct size measuring cup into the ingredient until it is full. Then level off the top of the cup with the flat side of a butter knife. Brown sugar is the only dry ingredient that should be tightly packed into a measuring cup.

- To measure liquid ingredients, such as milk and oil, use a clear glass or plastic measuring cup. Make sure it is on a flat surface. Pour the liquid into the cup until it reaches the correct level. Check the measurement at eye level.

- Remember that measuring spoons come in different sizes. Be sure you are using a *teaspoon* if the recipe asks for it and not a *tablespoon*.

Mixing:

- Beat—Mix ingredients together *fast* with a wooden spoon, whisk, or an electric mixer.

- Mix—Blend ingredients together with a wooden spoon, an electric mixer, or a whisk.

- Stir—Combine ingredients together with a wooden or metal spoon.

Cooking Terms

Cooking has its own vocabulary. Here are some terms you should be familiar with.

bread (verb)—To coat or cover with a layer of flour or crumbs before cooking.

brine—Water that is full of salt.

broth—A thin soup made by boiling meat, fish, or vegetables in water. Broth is also known as stock.

brown (verb)—To cook, usually in oil, until the food turns light brown.

chop (verb)—To cut into bite-sized pieces.

condiments—Foods that add a flavorful accent to a dish, such as mustard and tartar sauce.

cube (verb)—To cut into small cube-shaped pieces.

cuisine—The type of cooking used in a particular country.

dice (verb)—To cut into small pieces (smaller than chopped), about ¼-inch in size each.

drizzle (verb)—To pour a small amount of liquid in a stream over a dish.

fry—To cook in hot fat in a pan on top of the stove.

garnish—A bit of colorful food, such as parsley, that adds flavor to a dish and makes it look more attractive.

grate (verb)—To shred into small pieces with a grater.

grill (noun)—A cooking grate, used over a fire or burner.

grill (verb)—To broil or cook on a grate over a hot fire.

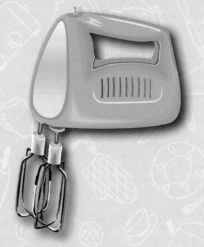

herbs—Plants such as oregano and basil, used to give food a distinctive flavor. They can be used fresh or dried.

marinate (verb)—To soak food in a liquid blend of seasonings (a marinade) so that it absorbs the flavors and becomes more tender.

mince (verb)—To chop into tiny pieces.

sauté (verb)—To fry lightly in a small amount of oil or fat.

savory—Highly flavored and tasty; not sweet.

seasonings—Ingredients used to bring out the flavor of a food, such as salt, pepper, herbs, and spices.

shred (verb)—To cut into small strips.

simmer (verb)—To cook over low heat just below the boiling point.

spice—A seasoning that has a strong or spicy aroma, for example, cinnamon or pepper.

staple—A main food item, needed nearly every day, such as flour or milk.

Cooking Tools

baking dish

colander

cutting board

cookie sheet

frying pan

juicer

measuring cups

grater

oven mitt

measuring spoons

pie pan

paring knife

potato masher

sieve

rolling pin

sauté pan

rubber spatula

slotted spoon

spatula

soup pot

whisk

vegetable peeler

Nutrition

The best food is healthy as well as delicious. In planning meals, keep in mind the guidelines of the food pyramid:

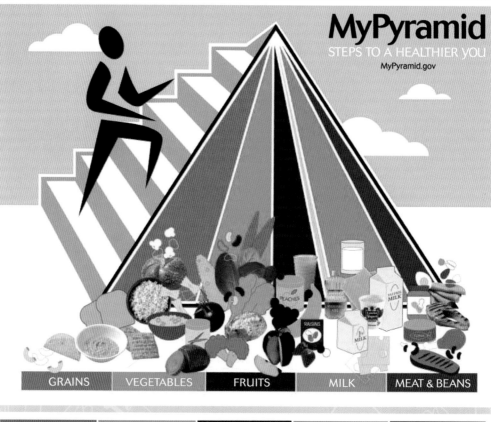

MyPyramid
STEPS TO A HEALTHIER YOU
MyPyramid.gov

GRAINS	VEGETABLES	FRUITS	MILK	MEAT & BEANS

GRAINS	VEGETABLES	FRUITS	MILK	MEAT & BEANS
Make half your grains whole	Vary your veggies	Focus on fruits	Get your calcium-rich foods	Go lean with protein
Eat at least 3 oz. of whole-grain cereals, breads, crackers, rice, or pasta every day	Eat more dark-green veggies like broccoli, spinach, and other dark leafy greens	Eat a variety of fruit	Go low-fat or fat-free when you choose milk, yogurt, and other milk products	Choose low-fat or lean meats and poultry
1 oz. is about 1 slice of bread, about 1 cup of breakfast cereal, or ½ cup of cooked rice, cereal, or pasta	Eat more orange vegetables like carrots and sweet potatoes	Choose fresh, frozen, canned, or dried fruit	If you don't or can't consume milk, choose lactose-free products or other calcium sources such as fortified foods and beverages	Bake it, broil it, or grill it
	Eat more dry beans and peas like pinto beans, kidney beans, and lentils	Go easy on fruit juices		Vary your protein routine — choose more fish, beans, peas, nuts, and seeds

For a 2,000-calorie diet, you need the amounts below from each food group. To find the amounts that are right for you, go to MyPyramid.gov.

Eat 6 oz. every day	Eat 2½ cups every day	Eat 2 cups every day	Get 3 cups every day; for kids aged 2 to 8, it's 2	Eat 5½ oz. every day

Conversions

Recipes list amounts needed. Sometimes you need to know what that amount equals in another measurement. And sometimes you may want to make twice as much (or half as much) as the recipe yields. This chart will help you.

DRY INGREDIENT MEASUREMENTS	
Measure	**Equivalent**
1 tablespoon	3 teaspoons
¼ cup	4 tablespoons
½ cup	8 tablespoons
1 cup	16 tablespoons
2 cups	1 pound
½ stick of butter	¼ cup
1 stick of butter	½ cup
2 sticks of butter	1 cup
LIQUID INGREDIENT MEASUREMENTS	
8 fluid ounces	1 cup
1 pint (16 ounces)	2 cups
1 quart (2 pints)	4 cups
1 gallon (4 quarts)	16 cups

Chapter 1

Sushi

Cold rice rolled in seaweed with vegetables, fish, or both in the middle—that's sushi (*SOO-shee*). Sushi came to Japan from China in the seventh century. Today, sushi is popular around the world.

Rice is very important in Japan. Japanese people can eat it three times a day. The word for breakfast, **asagohan**, means "first rice." The Japanese also eat a lot of seaweed. Japan celebrates National Seaweed Day in February.

Japan

Japan is a country in the Pacific Ocean. It is made up of four large islands, plus about three thousand small islands. Its land area is smaller than California. Japan is very mountainous. Food can be grown on only 15 percent of the land.

Nori

Nori (*NOR-ee*) is crispy, salty seaweed. It comes in thin, dried sheets, perfect for rolling things in. Farmers harvest seaweed from the ocean with nets. Then they shred and dry it on racks. Japan ships nori around the world. You can buy nori in many grocery stores.

What You Need

Equipment:
Saucepan with lid
Wooden spoon
Cutting board
Sharp knife
Plate

Ingredients:
1 cup **sushi rice**
1½ cups water
1 teaspoon salt
5–7 nori sheets
Cooked shrimp
Sliced cucumber (optional)
Sliced avocado (optional)

Garnish: Soy sauce, sesame seeds, pickled ginger, and **wasabi** paste

What's This?

Sushi rice, also called "shari," has short, fat grains. When cooked, sushi rice is stickier than regular rice.

What's This?

A bit of colorful food that adds flavor to a dish.

What's This?

Spicy green Japanese horseradish. You can buy wasabi and pickled ginger in most grocery stores.

What to Do
Cook the rice:

1. Boil water in saucepan.
2. Measure the rice and salt. Add to the boiling water.
3. Reduce heat to low and cover the pot.
4. Simmer the rice for 7–10 minutes.
5. Cover the rice. Let it cool for at least 10 minutes.

Cook's Tip

The rice is done when it is soft, not crunchy and not mushy.

Roll the Sushi:

1. Lay nori flat on the cutting board.
2. Wet your hands and spread rice on the nori.
3. At one end, set a row of cooked shrimp and other ingredients that you like.
4. Dip your fingers in water. Wet the ends of the nori.
5. Roll the nori with your fingertips and the palm of your hand.
6. Seal the edges closed with your damp fingertips. Chill in the refrigerator for two hours.
7. With a sharp knife, cut the long nori roll into slices about one inch thick.

Set the rolls on a plate. Garnish sushi with soy sauce, sesame seeds, pickled ginger, and wasabi paste.

Cook's Tip

Wet your fingers to spread the sticky rice.

Quesadillas

In Spanish, *queso* (*KAY-so*) means "cheese." A quesadilla (*kay-sah-DEE-yah*) is "a little cheesy thing." It is like a grilled cheese sandwich with a tortilla instead of bread.

Mexico

Mexico is the country just south of the United States. Mexico City, the capital, is the third-largest city in the world, after Tokyo and New York City. The world's smallest known volcano is in the town of Pueblo, Mexico. It is inactive and only 43 feet tall.

Tortillas

Torta means "plain round cake." In Mexico, tortillas (*tor-TEE-yuhs*) are a **staple**—a food used every day. They are served with most Mexican meals. Tortillas are used to make tacos, enchiladas, burritos, and other dishes. Traditionally, tortillas are made by hand from cornmeal and cooked over a fire.

What You Need

Equipment:
Grater
Frying pan
Spatula
Plate

Ingredients:
Tortillas
Cheese
1 teaspoon of oil or butter

Filling Options (choose 2 or 3):
Avocado, cut-up cooked chicken, sliced onion, jalapeño peppers, black olives, tomato, or red beans
▸ Salsa (you can use store-bought) or pico de gallo

Cook's Tip

Store-bought tortillas are great! Choose corn or flour, large or small.

Shred cheese with a grater. This will cut it into tiny strips. Shredded cheese melts faster.

What's This?

Salsa means "sauce." *Pico de gallo* means "rooster's beak." It is fresh salsa made from chopped tomato, onion, and chili peppers.

What to Do
Prepare it:

1. Layer shredded cheese on half of a tortilla.
2. (Optional) Top the cheese with other ingredients, if you choose. Don't overfill your quesadilla!
3. Fold the tortilla in half.

Grill it:

1. Put the oil or butter into the frying pan.
2. Heat the frying pan on medium heat.
3. Set the quesadilla into the hot pan by sliding it off the spatula.
4. Grill it for 1-2 minutes on each side. It should be golden brown. Watch it so it does not burn.
5. With the spatula, remove it from the pan. Set it on a plate. (Careful— its hot!)
6. When it cools a little, slice the quesadilla like a pie.
7. Eat it with your fingers. Dip it into salsa.

Serves 1.

Cook's Tip

Keep the plate nearby. You won't want to walk too far balancing the quesadilla on your spatula.

Chapter 3

Daal

Daal (*doll*) is bean soup or stew. It is served with rice and vegetables, or with flatbread for dipping. (***Chapatis***, ***naan***, and ***roti*** are types of Indian flatbread.) Daal is a staple dish in India as well as in Pakistan, Sri Lanka, Bangladesh, and Nepal. There are many recipes for daal. They all use the same basic ingredients—dried beans, liquid, and seasonings. The kind of beans and seasonings vary from region to region.

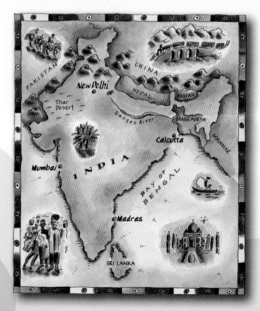

India

India is just a little bigger than Argentina, and about one-third the size of the United States. But it is the second-most populated country in the world (behind China), with over one billion people.

The Taj Mahal, one of the wonders of the world, was built in the 1600s. It is in the medieval city Agra, near India's capital, New Delhi. India's largest city is Mumbai, with a population of almost 14 million people.

Lentils and Spices

Lentils are dried beans from the legume family. They look like split peas. They come in red, brown, or yellow. They do not cost much. They are tasty, high in protein, and easy to cook.

Spices are key to Indian cooking. Spices like ginger, coriander, cumin (*CYOO-min*), turmeric (*TUR-mer-ik*), red chiles, and black mustard seeds are used in many Indian dishes.

What You Need

Equipment:
Strainer

Large saucepan with lid

Mixing spoon

Cutting board

Paring knife

Frying pan

Spatula

What to Do

1. Rinse lentils in a strainer.
2. Mix lentils and water in a saucepan on the stove.
3. Bring to a boil. Turn heat to low. Cover the saucepan.
4. Simmer until lentils are tender, 45 minutes to an hour. Stir often so the lentils do not burn.
5. Dice the onion and mince the garlic.
6. Heat oil in frying pan; add salt, pepper, cumin, turmeric, onion, and garlic to the pan.
7. Sauté (lightly fry) until onion is tender (about 5 minutes).
8. Scrape onion mixture into lentils. Simmer with the lid ajar for about 20 minutes. Stir often. Keep the lid half off to let steam escape. For soupy daal, add more water. For thick stew, simmer longer with the lid off.
9. Serve over cooked rice or with flatbread.

Serves 4–6.

Ingredients:
1 cup dried lentils

3 cups water

2 tablespoons vegetable oil

1 teaspoon salt

Ground pepper to taste

1 teaspoon ground cumin

1 teaspoon ground turmeric

1 onion

2 cloves garlic, minced ◄·····

Cooked rice (optional)

Flatbread (optional)

What's This?

A clove is one section of a garlic bulb. Take the papery skin off before using it.

Chapter 4

Tabouli

Tabouli (*tuh-BOO-lee*) is a salad with grain and herbs. Often, herbs are used just to season a dish. In tabouli, however, herbs are a main ingredient. Fresh green parsley and mint make the salad green and full of flavor. In Lebanon, tabouli is sometimes eaten by scooping it up with lettuce leaves.

Lebanon

Lebanon is the only Arab country that has no desert. The Republic of Lebanon (its official name) is a small country at the eastern end of the Mediterranean Sea and the western end of Asia. Its capital, Beirut, is right on the coast.

Lebanon has been inhabited since prehistoric times. Phoenicians were the first well-known group of people to live there.

Bulgur

Bulgur is a grain. It is cracked wheat. You can find it in the grocery store near rice and grains.

What You Need

Equipment:

Saucepan or kettle

Medium bowl

Paring knife

Cutting board

Jar or small bowl

Mixing spoon

Ingredients:

<u>For the salad</u>

1 cup bulgur

1 cup water

1 cucumber

1 tomato

2 green onions (also called scallions)

1 cup fresh parsley

¼ cup fresh mint

1 clove garlic

<u>For the dressing</u>

1 lemon

½ cup extra virgin olive oil

1 teaspoon salt

½ teaspoon pepper

What's This?

Olive oil is made by pressing olives. Extra virgin olive oil comes from the first pressing. It is the most flavorful.

What to Do

Part 1. Cook the bulgur:

1. Boil 1 cup of water in a saucepan or kettle.
2. Measure dry bulgur into a bowl.
3. Measure and pour hot water over the bulgur.
4. Let the bulgur sit for 30 minutes to absorb all the water.

Part 2. Chop the vegetables:

1. Cut the cucumber and tomato into bite-sized pieces.
2. Chop the green onions into small slices.
3. Remove the parsley leaves from the stems. Throw out the stems.
4. Mince the garlic and herbs—the fresh mint and parsley.

Part 3. Mix the dressing:

1. Cut the lemon in half.
2. Squeeze the juice into a bowl with a lemon juicer or with your hands. Remove the seeds!
3. Put the olive oil, salt, and pepper along with the lemon juice into a jar or bowl.
4. Shake or stir until the dressing is mixed.

Part 4. Make the salad:

1. Add the herbs and vegetables to the cooked bulgur.
2. Pour the dressing over the salad.
3. Stir with a mixing spoon.
4. Serve tabouli chilled or at room temperature.

What's This?

Chop into tiny pieces. The more you mince, the more flavor comes out! You can also use a food processor to mince the herbs and garlic.

Cook's Tip

The longer tabouli sits, the more flavor it has. Store leftovers in the refrigerator. Tabouli tastes great the next day too.

25

Chapter 5

Bánh mì

Bánh mì (*bahn mee*) are sandwiches. A crusty roll is brushed with mayonnaise and stuffed with meat and pickled vegetables. Vietnamese people have opened many bánh mì shops around the world, including many places in the United States.

Vietnam

Vietnam is a tropical country in Southeast Asia. It extends south from China in a long, narrow S-curve. Laos and Cambodia lie west of Vietnam, and the South China Sea lies to the east. Hanoi is the capital of Vietnam, and Ho Chi Minh City is the largest city.

Pickled Vegetables

When fresh vegetables steep in a brine, a liquid made with vinegar and salt, they are pickled. The brine preserves the vegetables and changes their flavor. Pickles are thought to be very healthy.

What You Need

Equipment:
Cutting board
Bread knife
Paring knife
Butter knife
Bowl
Plate

Ingredients:
Cucumber
Carrots
Radishes
Cabbage
French baguette (or your favorite sandwich roll)
Mayonnaise
Soy sauce
Cooked pork, ham, and/or chicken
Cilantro
Jalapeños (optional)

For brine:
¼ cup white vinegar
1 tablespoon granulated sugar
1 teaspoon kosher salt
Black pepper

Cook's Tip

Choose the veggies you like!

You can use leftovers or sandwich meats.

What to Do

Pickle the vegetables:

1. Slice cucumbers, radishes, cabbage, and carrots into thin slices.
2. Make the brine. Mix the vinegar, sugar, salt, and pepper in a bowl.
3. Add vegetables to the brine.
4. Let the veggies soak in the brine for 10–15 minutes up to 24 hours.

Cook's Tip

The longer the vegetables soak, the stronger they will taste.

Make the sandwich:

1. Slice the baguette in half lengthwise.
2. Spread a thin layer of mayonnaise on one or both sides.
3. Sprinkle some soy sauce on the bread.
4. Layer the bread with sandwich ingredients.
5. Coarsely chop cilantro. Sprinkle it on lettuce.
6. Add jalapeños if you like them.
7. Fold the sandwich over. Press it down. Cut it in half.

Serves 1

Pick it up and eat it!

Chapter 6

Fried Zucchini
with Yogurt Sauce

Yogurt is made by adding
healthy bacteria to milk. It is
thick, creamy, and slightly tangy.
It is often eaten with fruit. However,
the yogurt sauce in this recipe is savory—salty and tasty
rather than sweet. It can be eaten with salads, vegetables
(like zucchini), and meat such as chicken or fish.

Bulgaria

Bulgaria is a country in eastern
Europe that borders the Black
Sea. The cuisine of Bulgaria has
Middle Eastern, Turkish, and
Greek influences.

What You Need

Equipment:
Paring knife
Cutting board
2 small bowls
Frying pan
Spatula
Plate
Paper towels
Mixing spoon

Ingredients:
1 zucchini—medium or large
1 teaspoon salt
½ cup flour
½ cup oil (vegetable, canola, or olive oil)

For the sauce:
1 garlic clove
1 teaspoon minced fresh dill
1 cup plain, unflavored yogurt
Salt and black pepper to taste

Cook's Tip

If you like herbs, use chopped parsley too.

What to Do

Cook the zucchini:

1. Cut the stem ends off the zucchini. Cut zucchini into slices about ¹⁄₃ inch thick.
2. In a bowl, mix the flour and salt.
3. Dip zucchini slices into the flour, covering both sides. Set on plate.
4. Heat olive oil in frying pan until hot. Place zucchini slices in the oil. Fry 2 minutes. Flip slices carefully with spatula. Fry the other side 1 or 2 minutes until slices are light brown.
5. If the oil in the pan is too low, add more.
6. Lift slices from the frying pan with the spatula. Set them on a plate covered with a paper towel to soak up the extra oil.

For a thicker coating, bread the zucchini. First dip it into a bowl of milk or one beaten egg and then into the flour.

Be careful: Hot oil spatters! Don't stand too close to the pan. If the oil sizzles too much, turn the heat down.

Make the sauce:

1. Crush the garlic clove with a garlic press, or mince it with a sharp knife.
2. Mince fresh dill.
3. Measure yogurt into a bowl. Stir salt, pepper, garlic, and dill into the yogurt.
4. Serve fried zucchini warm. Dip slices into yogurt sauce.

Serves 4–6.

Chapter 7

Pyttipanna

In Swedish, *pyttipanna* (*pih-tee-PAH-nah*) means "small things in a pan." This popular lunch mixes pan-fried potatoes and meat. It is served with a fried egg on top.

Sweden

Sweden is part of the area called Scandinavia, along with Norway and Denmark. Northern Sweden is called "The Land of the Midnight Sun." In summer, north of the Arctic Circle, the sun never sets. Southern Sweden is called "Castle Land" because of all the castles, some from the fourteenth and fifteenth centuries.

Hash

The word *hash* means "jumble" or "mix." Many countries and regions in the United States have a version of hash. Most recipes combine meat and potatoes. Hash started as a way to use up leftovers. But hash is so good that it is often made fresh. Either way, it's delicious!

What You Need

Equipment:

Cutting board

Knife

Frying pan

Spatula

Ingredients:

4 cooked potatoes
(1 per person)

1 cup of meat—chicken,
 pork, turkey, or sausage

1 tablespoon olive oil

2 tablespoons butter,
divided

Salt and pepper, to taste

Optional: a dash of paprika, dry mustard, hot pepper flakes, or whatever seasonings you like

4 eggs (1 egg per person as desired)

Sliced pickled beets

Dill pickles

Cook's Tip

Try using fully cooked turkey bratwurst.

What to Do

Make the hash:

1. Cube the potatoes and meat.
2. Heat oil and 1 tablespoon butter in the frying pan.
3. Add potatoes.
4. Sprinkle with salt and pepper and other desired seasonings.
5. Sauté until light brown.
6. Add diced meat. Heat for 2-4 minutes. Stir frequently.
7. Scoop a portion onto each person's plate.

Fry the eggs:

1. Put 1 tablespoon of butter into the hot frying pan, the same one you used to cook the hash.
2. Crack the eggs into the melted butter.
3. Fry the eggs sunny-side up or over easy.

Assemble pyttipanna:

1. With the spatula, place an egg on top of each serving of hash.
2. Garnish pyttipanna with sliced pickled beets or dill pickle. **Serves 4.**

What's This?
Cut the ingredients into small cube-shaped pieces that are all about the same size.

Cook's Tip
How do you like your eggs? Sunny-side up eggs are fried only on one side. Over-easy eggs get flipped halfway through cooking.

Cook's Tip
Place beets or pickles on the side of the plate. The bright color makes it pretty. The vinegary taste complements the taste of the meat and potatoes.

Chapter 8

Sauerkraut Soup

You probably know the Hungarian word *goulash*. It means "stew." Hungarian cuisine features many stew and soup recipes. Sauerkraut soup is often served at midnight on New Year's Eve.

Hungary

Hungary is a small landlocked country in east-central Europe. It is bordered by the countries of Austria, Slovenia, Croatia, Serbia, Romania, Ukraine, and Slovakia. Hungary's capital city is Budapest which is located near the Danube River.

Paprika

Hungary is known for its paprika. Paprika is a spice made from ground dry red peppers. Paprika flavors range from mild and sweet to hot and spicy. Orange colored paprika is hotter (spicier) than red.

What You Need

Equipment:
Soup pot
Cutting board
Paring knife
Stirring spoon

Ingredients:
1 small onion
2 tablespoons vegetable or olive oil
About 1 cup of cooked sausage meat
1 tablespoon tomato paste
½ teaspoon powdered paprika
3-4 cups water or chicken stock
14-ounce can of sauerkraut
Salt and black pepper to taste
Pumpernickel or rye bread (optional)
Sour cream, butter, and/or cheese (optional)

What's This?
Kraut is cabbage. Sauerkraut means sour cabbage. It is made by fermenting shredded cabbage.

What to Do

1. Dice the onion.

2. Cube the sausage.

3. Heat oil in soup pot.

4. Sauté onion and sausage in oil for 3-4 minutes.

5. Add tomato paste and seasonings. Stir for 1 minute.

6. Add water or stock and sauerkraut.

7. Simmer soup, uncovered, for 10–15 minutes. Stir often.

8. Serve bowls of this hearty soup with pumpernickel or rye bread, with butter and cheese on the side. Top with a spoonful of sour cream if you want.

Serves 3-4.

Cook's Tip

This soup is supposed to be a little sour. If it is too sour, add a teaspoon of sugar. The sweetness will balance the sour taste.

Chapter 9

Arepas

Arepas (*ah-RAY-pahs*) are a flatbread, made like pancakes. Arepas are eaten plain, with butter, or stuffed with ham, cheese, or eggs. They can be grilled with chorizo (sausage). They can be a side dish for black beans, soup, stew, or meat.

Colombia

Colombia is a country on the northwest coast of the continent of South America. It is the only country on the continent with a coast along both the Atlantic Ocean and the Pacific Ocean.

Cornmeal

Arepas are made of cornmeal, a flour made by grinding dried corn. In Colombia and other South American countries, a cornmeal called masa is used to make tortillas and tamales.

What You Need

What's This?
Arepa flour is precooked cornmeal. Find it in a specialty grocery store.

Ingredients:

1 cup arepa flour OR ½ cup cornmeal plus ½ cup white flour

¼ pound mozzarella or cheddar cheese

¼–½ teaspoon salt

1 cup plus 2 tablespoons water

3 tablespoons vegetable oil

Equipment:

Grater

Bowl

Mixing spoon

Frying pan or cast-iron skillet

Spatula

Plate lined with waxed paper

Plate lined with paper towel

What to Do

1. Grate the cheese. You should have ½ cup to 1 cup.

2. In a bowl, mix the cornmeal, cheese, and salt.

3. Stir in water and mix until dough forms.

4. Let the dough rest for 1 to 2 minutes.

5. With your hands, scoop up about 3 tablespoons of dough.

6. Form a ball and flatten it in your palms, about the size of a hamburger bun.

7. Place the patty on waxed paper.

8. Form the rest of the dough into patties in the same way.

9. Pour the oil into your frying pan or skillet.

10. Heat it over medium heat until the oil shimmers.

11. Carefully place the dough patties into the pan.

12. Fry about 4 minutes on each side, turning them with a spatula, until the arepas are golden brown. If the oil gets low, add a little more.

13. Set them on a plate lined with a paper towel.

Makes about 4 arepas.

Wait until the arepas are cool enough to touch. Then eat them warm and fresh! Arepas should be crispy on the outside and moist in the middle.

Cook's Tip

With a few drops of water, keep your palms moist so the dough doesn't stick to your hands.

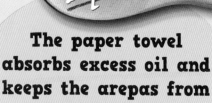

Cook's Tip

The paper towel absorbs excess oil and keeps the arepas from getting soggy.

Corn and Shrimp Soup

Brazilian cuisine has a lot of soup and stew recipes. Their cuisine is influenced by food from Portugal, France, Africa, and other countries.

Brazil

Brazil is the world's fifth-biggest country. It covers half of South America. Brazil was a colony of Portugal from 1500 to 1822. Portuguese is Brazil's official language. The capital city is Brasilia.

41

Marinade

A marinade is a liquid blend of seasonings. In this recipe, the shrimp are marinated. That means they steep in the marinade seasonings. They soak up the flavors.

What You Need

Equipment:
Bowl
Soup pot or saucepan
Cutting board
Paring knife
Stirring spoon
Spatula

Ingredients:
About 1 cup shrimp
¼ teaspoon garlic powder
1 tablespoon lemon juice
1 teaspoon salt
Black pepper, to taste
1 onion, small to medium
3 tablespoons olive oil
1 cup frozen corn kernels
1 tablespoon cilantro
3 cups chicken stock or water

Cook's Tip

You can use shrimp that are fresh and raw or frozen and fully cooked. Buy them already peeled and deveined. If they are "tails-on," it is easy to pull the tails off the shrimp.

What to Do

1. In a bowl, mix the shrimp with garlic powder, lemon, and salt and pepper. Let it marinate while you make the rest of the soup.

2. Dice the onion. Finely chop the cilantro.

3. Heat oil in soup pot or saucepan.

4. Sauté onion in oil for 3-4 minutes.

5. Add cilantro.

6. Add corn and stock. Stir. Bring soup to a boil. Lower heat and simmer for 7–10 minutes.

7. Add seasoned shrimp.

8. If using raw shrimp, cook until shrimp are done, about 2½ minutes per side.

9. If using frozen cooked shrimp, thaw before using. Heat gently in soup for 1 minute.

Serves 4.

cilantro

Cook's Tip

Using a rubber spatula, scrape the flavors from the bowl into the soup.

Cook's Tip

Be careful not to overcook. Shrimp get rubbery if they cook too long.

Chapter 11

Mousetraps

Mouestraps are open-faced grilled cheese sandwiches. New Zealanders call any kind of toasted sandwiches "toasties." Why are these toasties called mousetraps? The cheese, of course!

New Zealand

New Zealand is a remote island country in the Pacific Ocean. Its closest neighbor is Australia, 1,250 miles away. You can see New Zealand's beautiful landscape in movies filmed there, like the "Lord of the Rings" trilogy.

Marmite

Marmite is a salty spread made from yeast. A similar product is called Vegemite, from Australia. Marmite and Vegemite are often eaten on buttered toast. Marmite has a strong flavor. As popular as Marmite is in New Zealand, even New Zealanders either love the taste or hate it. The trick is to spread it on thinly. A little goes a long way.

What You Need

Equipment:
Cookie sheet
Butter knife
Grater
Small bowl
Fork

Ingredients:
4 slices bread
Butter
1 teaspoon Marmite or Vegemite—about ¼ teaspoon per slice
1 chunk of cheddar cheese, to make about 1 cup grated
1 egg (optional)

What's This?
You decide whether to use it or not. Mousetraps are great with just cheese.

What to Do

1. Toast bread in toaster, toaster oven, or under the oven broiler.
2. Butter the toast.
3. Thinly spread Marmite or Vegemite on each piece of toast.
4. Shred the cheese.
5. Crack the egg into a small bowl. Beat it with a fork.
6. Mix shredded cheese with egg.
7. Spread cheese mixture evenly on each slice of toast. Set the "toasties" on the cookie sheet.
8. Place in the oven broiler or toaster oven until the cheese melts.
9. Remove tray from oven.
10. Cut mousetraps into triangles or strips.

Cook's Tip

Start with a dab of Marmite on the end of your knife. You can add more if you like.

Cook's Tip

Use a cheese grater. Skip this step if you are using shredded cheese from the store.

What's This?

The broiler is the oven's hottest setting. It browns casseroles, broils meat, and melts cheese. To use, place the oven rack close to the broiler when the oven is cool, then turn it on.

Further Reading

Books

Behnke, Alison, with Vartkes Ehramjian. *Cooking the Middle Eastern Way: Culturally Authentic Foods Including Low-fat and Vegetarian Recipes.* Minneapolis, Minn.: Lerner Publications, 2005.

D'Amico, Joan, and Karen Eich Drummond. *The Coming to America Cookbook: Delicious Recipes and Fascinating Stories from America's Many Cultures.* Hoboken, N.J.: Wiley, 2005.

De Mariaffi, Elisabeth. *Eat It Up! Lip-Smacking Recipes for Kids.* Toronto: Owlkids, 2009.

Dodge, Abigail Johnson. *Around the World Cookbook.* New York: DK Publishing, 2008.

Lagasse, Emeril. *Emeril's There's a Chef in My World!: Recipes That Take You Places.* New York: HarperCollins Publishers, 2006.

Wagner, Lisa. *Cool Sweets & Treats to Eat: Easy Recipes for Kids to Cook.* Edina, Minn.: ABDO Publishing Co., 2007.

Internet Addresses

Cookalotamus Kids
<http://www.cookalotamus.com/kids.html>

PBS Kids: Café Zoom
<http://pbskids.org/zoom/activities/cafe/>

Spatulatta.com
<http://www.spatulatta.com/>

Index